TURNED

TABLES

MEMOIRS OF A SURVIVOR

Letta Lane

TURNED TABLES: MEMOIRS OF A SURVIVOR

The following is nonfiction. Real names have not been used.

I dedicate this book to my family. Thank you for supporting me throughout this journey.

TURNED TABLES: MEMOIRS OF A SURVIVOR

Prologue

My children don't often ask me about their father. Maybe it's because they're grown now, and they somehow knew not to ask when they were younger. I loved him. And my children are here because of him. Maybe I forgave him because of them.

Chapter One

It was October 1966 in Gary, Indiana and I was working at a daycare for children with disabilities. At the daycare, I assisted the children who needed help doing things that other children could do for themselves, like using the bathroom and feeding themselves. The nurses at the daycare would set up activities and games for the children to do. Part of my job was to play these games with the children and guide them through the activities. I really enjoyed my time with these children. Their disabilities ranged from needing a helping hand to needing everything done for them. The nurses would watch how I cared for the children and always complimented me on my kindness and patience. One of the nurses went so far as to say that I should be a nurse because I was caring and because I worked well with the kids. I had always wanted to be a nurse so when she said this to me it made me feel wonderful about myself.

I worked at the day care in the mornings and in the afternoons, I'd ride with my co-worker Mary to Manpower where we took classes. We learned how to type, how to use an all-transistorized calculator, the first desk calculator that used transistors, and we were trained to be cashiers. Most of the women in the workforce during that time had to know these skills to even be considered for any level of position within a company.

Even though I only worked at the daycare half of the day, I was always tired and my feet were often sore from standing for long periods of time. On one particular day, we had left the daycare and were on our way to class. Mary was driving and I was in the passenger seat. Sam, another co-worker, was in the back. Mary tuned the radio a couple of times before we heard the Temptation's "Ain't too Proud to Beg" come on.

We started singing and grooving. Ahh! The Temptations! There were five of them and they were one of the best groups during that time. Eddie Kendricks was my favorite because he could reach the high notes. I remember trying to reach those notes like him and I thought I came pretty close to it. Not only did I love to listen to them sing, but I loved to watch them dance. I had seen them perform many times at the Regal theater in Chicago and I always enjoyed their choreography.

We were driving along and as we were approaching a stop light, it turned yellow so Mary slowed down and then the light turned to red. There was a bus stop on the right. Mary turned and said to me "I know him, roll down your window". I reached for the handle and cranked it until the window went down. She leaned and yelled out the window and asked the man if he wanted a ride. Louis was handsome and mature looking. He was average height with a caramel complexion and chiseled facial features. He said yes, tossed his cigarette down, and got in the back seat sitting directly behind me. As we continued driving I could feel the stares on the back of my head.

The Temptations were fading out when he leaned forward and said that he wasn't too proud to beg for my phone number. I laughed, pulled out some paper and a pen from my purse, and wrote my number down. Mary dropped Louis off and the rest of us went to class.

Louis called me that night and asked me to dinner. I told my parents about meeting Louis and that we were going to dinner. My mother was thrilled. I had dated other men before but those relationships never worked out. I was going to be 21 next month and during those days by the age of 20 most girls were married and had children already.

The next day the doorbell rang and I felt butterflies in my stomach. I went to the door and opened it and there he was, this handsome man. I let him in and introduced him to my family. He was very charming and I could tell that my mother and father really liked him. My mother was all smiles as she told us to have a good time at dinner. I grabbed my coat and we left. Louis didn't have a car and it wasn't a big deal to ride the city bus to get around, so we walked to the bus stop and talked until the bus pulled up. We talked and laughed the whole bus ride to the restaurant.

Louis was 10 years my senior. He'd been to college, where he studied pre-med, but he had dropped out before he could finish. I never asked him why he dropped out, but I never doubted him about actually going because I could tell that he was very smart. He also served in the Navy. I was really intrigued with his life experiences and I wanted to know more. We arrived at the restaurant and we talked and laughed some more. There was never a pause or an awkward moment that night. We both were into each other, it was as if there weren't any other people around. On the bus ride home Louis told me that he'd like to see me again and that this time he would cook for me.

The next time Louis came to get me, he was driving his brother's car. He opened the door for me and we drove to his place. He'd crack the window while he smoked his cigarettes and in-between puffs we'd talk.

He lived in an attic apartment in a house that belonged to a married couple. I thought it was a nice place. There was a stairway from the outside leading up to the attic. It was much like a studio apartment. The stove was the first thing I saw when he opened the door. The apartment was clean and tidy. There were Macramé hangers with artificial plants in them. My eyes were immediately drawn to the dark oak panels surrounding the apartment. I thought this was a nice touch for an apartment. I noticed a record player and several stacks of Jazz albums. Louis loved jazz. Some of his favorite jazz artists were Jimmy Smith, Jimmy Mcgriff, and Yusef Lateef. He also had a lot of medical and sociology text books.

He turned the TV on and we watched different television shows while he cooked. He liked to watch Star Trek, a show about a crew completing missions in space. It wasn't my favorite, but I'd watch it. My favorite shows were Bonanza and Gunsmoke, because my father would watch these and other westerns all the time. After a while, a delicious scent started to fill the air. We sat down to eat at the table and to my surprise the food was delicious. He was handsome, mature, and he could cook. I felt really good about this. He was always a gentleman, he complimented me and made me feel good about myself.

We courted for several weeks. I'd go to his apartment and we'd watch TV, or we'd go to the movies. We were inseparable. One day I went over to Louis' apartment and his brother Sam and Sam's wife were there. He introduced me to them as his lady. His brother pulled out some marijuana. He and Louis smoked it while I talked to Sam's wife. I thought that she was a nice lady. She seemed a little anxious though.

Another time I went over to Louis' house his sister had dropped by and they smoked marijuana together. I told him that it didn't bother me. From that day on Louis was not shy about smoking marijuana in front of me. I didn't feel like it was that big of a deal because I was around people who smoked marijuana all the time and it was just something that people did. I knew that just because they smoked it, it didn't mean that I had to.

Louis was a good talker. He was very clear and articulate with his words. He continued to open up to me. He told me that when he was 4 his mother died and that he and his brother went to live with his father's brother in Mississippi. His sister went to live with his aunt in Michigan. I never asked him why he didn't just stay with his father, but I wondered. He said that his uncle was mean to him and that he beat him all the time. I felt really sad for Louis and it made me feel special that he would share this sensitive information with me. I was drawn to him.

He mentioned a little bit about his time in the Navy. I know that he enlisted in March 1957. He spoke of a time when he cursed out a sergeant and implied that he was sent to Korea for doing so. Ironically, while in Korea, he became a drill sergeant. He received an honorable discharge in August of 1961.

He also said that he played college basketball, but he didn't like to talk much about his college days. I didn't feel that his past was important, so I never asked him to tell me more.

The days were getting colder and I needed a fancy coat to wear when we went out. Louis took me shopping and bought me a suede coat. It was long, medium brown, form fitting at the top and it flared at the bottom. We would go shopping together from time to time because he liked for me to wear nice things.

My days were busy with the daycare, classes, and spending time with Louis. I saw an advertisement in the paper about a class for IBM key punching. I felt that if I was a keypunch operator that I'd be able to stay off my feet and I wouldn't be so exhausted at the end of the day. The only problem was that I didn't have the money for the classes. When I told Louis about this, he said not to worry, that he would pay for it. I was very excited because during that time keypunch operators were in high demand. That type of technology was used in all industries and the pay was pretty good.

December came and I was in love. I had never felt like this before. I thought about Louis day and night. I was 21 now and I felt the pressure to start a family. I was delighted when Louis asked me to marry him. People that he knew saw us together all the time and they suggested that we get married. He asked me and then asked my parents. I think that my mother was as happy as I was. She was very active at her church and was told by a fellow church member once, that every woman my age should be married with children. Even though my mother never put pressure on me directly to get married, I could tell that she really wanted me to.

We went shopping that very next day for a ring. We drove to Chicago and Louis bought my engagement ring at Comays Jewelers. It was a Marquise diamond that I still have to this day. Louis said that I could quit my job and stop taking classes at Manpower because he was going to take care of me. I was overjoyed with the idea of staying home and taking care of him.

We didn't waste any time. We got married that same month at my parent's house. My brothers and sisters were very excited. I was the eldest of 10 and I knew they were ready for me to leave. The reverend at my mother's church that we had been going to since we moved to Gary married us. I was eager to make this covenant with Louis and God. After the wedding, we had the reception in the basement of one of my mother's good friends. It was a beautiful day.

Chapter Two

I packed all the things I had at my parents and brought them to Louis', now our, apartment. I liked that I didn't have to worry about furniture and that Louis had a good job working for Ford Motor Company. I no longer worked or took classes, so I had a lot of time on my hands. This proved to be trying because I had worked consistently since I was 16. Louis would go to work and I'd visit with the neighbors about whatever was going on in the news and in the neighborhood.

Louis bought an old Chevrolet, so that he didn't have to borrow his brother's car or catch the bus. Also, this way he could also get home faster. I would make sure that I had his food waiting for him when he came home from work. This was how I grew up. My mother always made breakfast for my dad before he went to work, she packed his lunch in a metal lunch container, and had dinner waiting for him after a long day's work at the steel mill. When I was a child I would often imagine myself doing the same thing.

When it came to paying the bills, Louis would pay them sometimes and other times he'd give me the money to pay them, and after I'd pay them there would barely be anything left. This was ok, but I wanted to get a job and earn my own money so that I could buy some of the things that I wanted. I liked to decorate so I would've loved to have bought things for the apartment. I also needed money to get my hair done and shop for clothes, things that made me feel good.

We did a lot together. We went shopping, to the movies, to jazz concerts, and to night clubs. Sometimes I'd see some of my old male classmates and Louis acted jealous. He didn't say anything, but I could tell by the change in his demeanor that he wasn't happy about me knowing other men. When we'd go to the night club, we'd just talk and sit and watch others because Louis didn't dance. I would've liked to have danced, but I was happy just being there with him.

Martha, one of my oldest friends, came to the apartment one day. We had a lot of catching up to do, so she was there for a while. It was nice to be able to see an old friend. Martha was still there when Louis came home. I didn't have dinner ready yet because Martha and I were talking and I'd lost track of time. He said rudely "get up and fix me some food". I was flustered. I didn't know what to say to Martha. One minute we were laughing and having a good time and then in an instant it turned sour. I couldn't believe that he would be so rude. She said that she had to go, but I don't think that was the truth. I think that she felt sorry for me. After she left, Louis talked about her so badly and for the life of me I couldn't understand where this was coming from. He called her ugly and fat. I never saw or heard from Martha again.

I was skeptical about inviting friends over after that, but I convinced myself that maybe Louis was just having a bad day the day that Martha came over. I asked another one of my friends to come by and visit. This time Louis was home. Everything seemed to be going ok, we were all having a good time laughing and listening to his jazz albums. When she left, Louis tried to make it seem like she was a tramp. He said that she was dressed promiscuously and that she kept giving him inviting looks. He confessed that he touched her inappropriately to keep her from coming back to the house. We argued about this, because it didn't make any sense to me. I felt that he had betrayed me. I didn't want to invite anyone over anymore.

I didn't drive, so Louis would take me wherever I needed to go. There was a time when he dropped me off at the beauty shop. When he came to pick me up he had his brother Sam with him. My beautician was a man and although this wasn't rare, it wasn't common in our area. Louis and Sam started calling him names. They called him gay and used other offensive names to describe him. I was so embarrassed to hear them say these things that I never went back to that beautician to get my hair done. After Louis dropped Sam off at his house, we went home and we argued about how cruel I felt that he and his brother were acting.

One day I had just finished cleaning up the kitchen after having fixed dinner, when there was a knock on the door. It was the woman who owned the house. She said that we were making too much noise in the kitchen and she asked us to move out. Too much noise? I was preparing meals often, which required me to use a lot of dishes, therefore I had a lot of dishes to wash and put away. I thought that I was making normal noise. I've often wondered if there was something more behind her asking us to leave.

We moved in with his brother Sam. He lived by himself in a 3-bedroom house, so there was plenty of room for us. Within the time of Louis and I getting married and moving in with Sam, Sam's wife had divorced him and took their twins to a small town in Michigan. Louis explained that Sam used to beat his wife and that's why she left him and moved back to Michigan. The good thing was that we didn't have much to move, just our clothes and kitchen items.

I believe that Louis was jealous of Sam because they argued all the time. He didn't like for his brother to say anything to me at all. Louis would tell him not to talk to me. I was annoyed by this and felt it quite controlling. Louis told me that his uncle and aunt that raised them favored Sam, because they always said that Sam was smart. Sam was an electrician by trade and a very good one. One day, the city turned off the electricity because he didn't pay the electric bill. Sam climbed up the pole, switched the wires around, and turned the electricity back on.

Louis and his brother smoked marijuana every day. There were a lot of men coming over at all hours of the day and night. They would stop by, but they wouldn't stay very long. I finally realized that Sam was a drug dealer. I felt on edge staying there. I was uncomfortable and after a lot of complaining and arguing with Louis about this, we finally moved out.

My aunt Evelynn, had a house for rent so we moved in there. It was a 1-story house and there were roaches everywhere, but we didn't have any other options. We had to have it exterminated. I was just glad that I was finally able to get Louis to agree to move out of his brother's house. Our new home had a big living room and 2 bedrooms. All the places that we had lived in so far already had furniture. Aunt Evelynn's house was completely empty, so we had to go shopping to fill it. I found a nice living room set, a kitchen set, and a bedroom set. We went to the counter to apply for store credit and to my surprise Louis was declined. I had no idea that his credit was bad, so I applied to be a cosigner for the furniture and luckily, we were able to purchase it all and have it delivered.

His sister and her 3 kids would come by and visit us sometimes. One day I discovered that they were no longer just smoking marijuana, they were snorting cocaine. I was furious. I couldn't believe that this was the man I had married. I started to feel downhearted. I wondered what I had gotten myself into. I didn't hold my tongue. If I wasn't happy or didn't agree with something Louis and I would argue about it. I later found out that his sister's boyfriend was the one supplying them with the drugs (he was also her pimp).

I remember one time when the boyfriend laid out all the cocaine that he had for them on the table. He had it on some paper and made lines with it using a razor blade. Louis and his sister would take it into her bedroom while I waited in the living room. I never saw the boyfriend using with them. He made it a point to show me how many lines could kill a person. I think he felt that if I knew, that I'd be willing to try it. Louis tried to get me to do it, but I refused, and this made him angry. He wanted me to be ok with it, so I wouldn't complain about him spending money on it.

Louis also had a friend who was a dentist that he would get high with. He and this dentist would go to the marijuana fields and steal the marijuana and sell it. They were really good friends and I argued with Louis about stealing the drugs and selling them. I didn't understand what was going on with Louis. I kept going back to the covenant that I made on my wedding day.

Louis had lost his job at Ford and was upset about it, so he was on edge and quick to argue. Soon after he lost his job, he started working for my uncle Ken doing construction. He had a lot of job assignments and was rarely at home now. We could talk without arguing. I was seeing more of the man that I married.

Even though he wasn't at home much, his sister would stop by with her kids. I didn't like this because they didn't know how to behave, they would tear things up. They'd take my records and throw them on the floor. I told Louis about this and he got really mad insinuating that I didn't want his people over. One day when I complained he got so angry that he snatched the door off the hinges and kicked our glass table and broke it. I was shaken up and all those uneasy feelings that I had before came back.

Another time that I complained about his sister and her kids, he choked me and threatened to kill me. I couldn't believe that this had just happened. I was terrified and I didn't know what to do. I had prayed that things would get better, surely this was not God's plan for me.

As soon as Louis went to sleep I went to my mother's house and told her what happened. She offered for me to come back home and stay. I remained at my parents until Louis came looking for me. He came to the house yelling and screaming and when I refused to go, he threatened to hurt my mother and she panicked. She told me that she was worried about me but didn't want me to come back there again because she was afraid that Louis would hurt her. I felt alone and heavyhearted. I couldn't go home so I stayed with Louis.

Louis would often say that he didn't want any kids because he had planned to go back to college, but when I became pregnant with Terri, he seemed to be happy. Maybe this was what we needed to get things back to the way they were in the beginning. We went shopping and bought a few things for the baby; things were good. Terri was born in 1969.

Our contentment didn't last long. Things started to get worse again when Louis' sister's boyfriend was killed. The reports said that someone shot him in a crowd and that he was not the intended target. She lost her job as a legal secretary and she and her 3 kids moved in with us. Louis would take money that we needed to pay the bills to buy cocaine and heroin for him and his sister. He never yelled at her kids for being loud or for breaking anything.

Louis couldn't stand to hear Terri cry. He'd take his belt off and pull her panties down and spank her bare bottom. There would be welts on her bottom. My heart sank every time I'd see him start to take off his belt. I'd jump to Terri's defense every time. We would then start fighting. He wasn't very strong and because I grew up with 7 brothers, he couldn't get the best of me.

Even though Louis wasn't raised by his father, his father was still in his life. I remember a time that his father came to visit us, to see Terri. Sam, his brother, came by as well. They started reminiscing about the past and all of sudden

Louis and Sam started throwing punches. Their father had to break it up. These grown men had been fighting about something that happened when they were little. He never told me what he and his brother were actually fighting about.

As Terri got older and she began to walk, she was very active. She was always running and jumping off of things. She jumped off the couch one day and busted her eyebrow. I got really nervous and was scared to say anything to Louis. It was an open cut and blood was gushing everywhere. I could tell that she needed stiches. Luckily, Louis seemed concerned too, so we took her to the emergency room and she got stiches.

I was pregnant again and I started having this excruciating tooth pain. I went to Louis' friend, the dentist, for a tooth extraction. He said that he had to take an x-ray and he didn't cover my stomach. When I reached about 6 months in my pregnancy I couldn't feel the baby move. I began to feel worried and anxious. Then I started having pains, so I called the doctor and got in to see him right away. That's when he gave me the worse news ever. The doctor told me that the baby wasn't moving and that he couldn't hear a heartbeat. I was heartbroken. I cried and cried and cried and I did not understand why this had happened. I was sinking further and further into to a pit of despair. I didn't think that I could get any more depressed. The doctor suggested that I deliver the baby. So, I did.

After our baby was delivered, Louis' father came to visit. It seemed to help Louis simply because his dad was there. Even though Louis appeared to be upset about the death of our baby, I always had doubts in my mind that his sadness was genuine. One day I was reading one of my health magazines and I came across an article that showed research claiming that women who had dental work while pregnant ran the risk of a stillbirth. I know that Louis seemed to be upset but I still couldn't help but wonder if he and his dentist friend conjured this plan up to kill our baby on purpose.

Not too long after the death of our baby we got the news that Sam was killed. He was in a hit and run accident. Louis and his brother had their issues, but they were really close. This was the blow that made Louis' temper much worse. Terri was almost 2 years old when this happened. He was so enraged all the time and I felt that I was always walking on eggshells.

Louis decided that he was going to get a dog. He decided that he would teach the dog how to attack. He bought the dog a collar and put it on tightly around the dog's neck. When he'd walk him, he'd yank hard on the leash. The dog would bleed around the neck. This made me infuriated and we'd argue and fight about it. My aunt Evelyn and some of the neighbors saw the dog and they threatened to call the police on him. I remember him telling my aunt that he had a gun. She said to him "so what, everyone has one of those." The threat of the police didn't change anything. He continued to choke the dog every day with the dog collar and leash and we'd argued about it every day.

I was so upset about this not only because I felt it was wrong, but because Terri would see the dog bleeding and she'd cry. I told aunt Evelyn that he hadn't stopped choking the dog. She came by the house to confront Louis. They exchanged words and she told us we had to move.

The next place we moved into was a newly built apartment complex. His sister and her kids were still living with us at aunt Evelyn's when she told us to move, so they moved into the apartment with us too. They didn't stay with us at the apartment for very long because they found a place just across the state line in Michigan and moved there.

Louis was extremely sad when they moved. He was more depressed than ever before and he was inconsolable. I think that he missed getting high with his sister. He started to arrive late to a couple of jobs sites, so my uncle fired him. He didn't seem too concerned about this because he had decided that we'd just move to Michigan and that he'd get a job there. A new place. Maybe a new start is what we needed.

Chapter Three

We left Indiana and moved to Bangor, Michigan, which was about 95 miles east of Gary. The first place that we stayed at was a motel. It was small but decent. Louis got a job with a construction company. While working on a job he met a man who had some houses for rent. This man was a millionaire. He raced horses and made a lot of money doing so. He owned a lot of land on which he and his wife built a mansion and close to the mansion there were several smaller homes. We went to look at the property and it wasn't bad at all. The grass was overgrown on several parts of the land and it was growing wildly, but that was an easy fix. We decided to rent the property.

I missed my family in Indiana. When we lived there I felt like I had their support, but now that we were in Michigan I didn't have my family to talk to whenever Louis and I would argue. It was only an hour and a half drive between Bangor and Gary, so we would still go back and forth. I didn't drive so I needed Louis to go with me every time I wanted to go to visit my family and friends. The short distance made it doable for Louis' friends to come and visit him too.

The dentist came to visit one time and noticed that there was wild grass growing. He and Louis felt that it resembled marijuana, so they started cutting it down and picking the weeds. They put it into the oven to curate it and then the dentist took it back to Gary to sell it.

This only happened one time because not too long after that there was an incident at the dentist's office. He was in his office getting high. He had gotten so high that when a woman came to check on him, he freaked out and shot and killed her. People said that he went crazy after that, that he would undress himself for no reason. I wondered if this was part of his plan to make others think that he was crazy so that he wouldn't be charged with killing the lady. It was rumored that his family sent him away down south somewhere to avoid going to jail. I still held resentment for what I believed the dentist did to my baby.

My youngest sister was getting into a lot of trouble and my mother asked if she could come and stay with us. I asked Louis and he laughed. He said that he wouldn't allow it. I kept pressuring him about it, after all, his sister and her kids lived with us before. Why couldn't my sister live with us too. He didn't like for me to question him. Out of nowhere, he pushed me down and choked me. That took me by surprise because I thought that things had gotten better. This was enough. I was so fearful, so I called my mom and asked her if I could come home, I told her that I wanted out of this terrible relationship. I was nervous about what she would say. I thought that she might tell me no because of what had happened before when I left Louis and sought refuge at her house. I was relieved when she said to come home.

I called a taxi after Louis had went to sleep. As soon as it arrived, I grabbed Terri and snuck out of the house. We took the taxi to the Greyhound bus stop and we rode the bus to

Gary. My parents were at the bus stop to pick us up. I was happy to see my parents, but yet I couldn't shake the sadness that I felt in my heart.

My solace was short-lived because Louis came to get me. This time my dad was there too. Louis threatened that he would kill us all if I didn't go back with him. I couldn't let that happen. I didn't want to see anyone get hurt. I had to go back with him. I was defeated.

My mother was worried sick about me. She thought it would be a good idea for my brother Johnny to come and stay with me and Louis. She believed that Johnny would be able to protect me. I asked Louis and thankfully he agreed. I felt a little safer with Johnny there even though I still cried myself to sleep every night. One day Johnny told me he was leaving and going back to Gary. Instantly, I felt the fear rushing back into my body. He must've gotten into it with Louis. He said he couldn't stay there because Louis had a bad attitude.

It had been a while since Louis tried to whip Terri. One day she had hurt herself and she started crying. He couldn't stand to hear it. He took off his belt and whipped her with it. I loathed the way he abused her, so every time I would come to her defense and we would argue. The arguments would escalate into fights. He would jump on me and I'd fight back and eventually fight him off. He began to realize that I was not going to back down, that I was not going to just sit there and let him whip Terri and this made him furious. I think this really played on his ego because from now on when we argued and fought he would go and grab his gun and he'd threaten to shoot me with it. He'd put it in my face. This would demoralize me and I'd back down. I understood now that this gave him a sense of power over me.

We had a butane stove in this house and I didn't know how to use it. One time I was about to cook something, so I turned the nozzle on the stove, but the stove didn't turn on. I was wondering why it wouldn't turn on, so I asked Louis if he knew. Several moments had passed and Louis gave me a match and told me to go light it. When I lit the match over the burner, it blew up in my face and it singed all the hair on my face. My eyebrows and my eyelashes were gone. I was in shock, but Louis didn't seem concerned. He didn't ask me if I was ok, he didn't rush over to check on me. When I looked at him he had this evil sinister look on his face. After I realized what had just happened, I was furious. I could've gotten seriously burnt. We argued about it. We went back and forth. Then he hit me so hard that he knocked me across the bed. All I could do was cry.

It was only later that Louis told me that you're supposed to light the match to start the stove right away and not to wait too long to light it. I now became conscious of the fact that he was capable of anything. I wondered if he even cared about me.

Louis' dad lived in Saginaw, Michigan. We decided to go and visit him one day. It was a long drive, about 3 hours. Terri still had a lot of energy and she was always moving around. When we got to his dad's house Louis wanted Terri to sit still, but she wouldn't listen. He took off his belt and I could feel my body stiffen up. He was about to whip her when his dad stopped him and told him not to. He said that it wasn't a good thing to do. He tried to explain to Louis that whipping children could have a bad effect on them, so Louis put the belt down and he didn't whip her there.

When we got back home, I could tell that what his father said went in one ear and out the other, because he continued to whip Terri. We continued to fight about it. He continued to get his gun and threaten me with it.

We had to move out of the house across from the mansion because Louis got into an argument with the millionaire's wife. He was mowing the lawn and he didn't do it the way she wanted him to, so she told him to move out. I think that there was more to that story though.

We then moved into Louis' aunt Lillian's cottage. Aunt Lillian was his father's sister. The cottage was in Bangor too, so we didn't have to move far. We moved all of our things into the cottage. I was hopeful that this change could be a new beginning for us. I was setting up the furniture and organizing things how I wanted them, while Louis was hanging all the pictures on the wall. There was a picture that he had hung that was crooked and I told him about it. He got extremely irate and was cursing up a storm. He got so mad and he went and got his gun. He was waving the gun, cursing, and threatening to kill me with it. I was arguing back and that's when he put the gun in my mouth. I was paralyzed. The other times that he had threatened me I never thought he would go through with it, but this time I thought that he might. He was so loud, that his aunt heard him as she was walking by. She came in the house and pleaded with him to give her the gun. Louis eventually gave her the gun. She told me to be careful—that he just might try to kill me. I was trembling and overwhelmed with despair.

I called my mom and pleaded with her to let me come home. I was desperate, I had to get me and my daughter away from this. She suggested that I go and stay with my aunt Gwen in Milwaukee, Wisconsin. I had two aunts that lived in Milwaukee, Gwen and Carolyn. The next day, while Louis was asleep my aunts put me and Terri on the bus to Milwaukee. Terri knew that we were leaving and would be gone for a while, so she grabbed her favorite doll. My nerves were so bad until the bus started going. We hadn't been seated very long when Terri said, "Mommy are you leaving daddy?" The people on the bus laughed and I was embarrassed. They had no idea what I had been going through. We stayed with my aunt Gwen and my other aunt Carolyn each for a couple days. They were concerned that I was suffering from depression, so they admitted me to the psychiatric ward in the hospital and watched Terri for me while I was in there. Louis was looking for me and he was relentless. He went to my mom and dad and threatened to kill them if they didn't tell him where I was. My mother eventually told him that I was in Milwaukee.

I had been at the hospital for a couple of days when Louis and his friend Steve found me there. Steve was the one that Louis would buy his marijuana from. Steve did most of the talking because he was calmer than Louis. Louis was angry and agitated. They talked to someone, who said that they weren't going to release me. This made Louis even more irate. He started yelling and cursing and he threated to bomb the hospital. They didn't even call the police they just let me go. I had lost all hope.

I went back to Michigan with him to more hell. I had nowhere safe to go. I continued to pray every day that God would help me and my child. When we got back to Bangor, he admitted me into the hospital, stating that I was mentally deranged. He took Terri to my mother's house in Gary. While I was in the hospital I found out that I was pregnant.

I wasn't in the hospital very long. Louis came and got me and then went to Gary to pick up Terri. My mother was concerned that I was pregnant again, so she suggested that I come to Gary for all my doctor's visits. Bangor was a small town and Louis didn't trust the physicians there too much. We had heard of stories about how a lot of people had died because they didn't get the care that they needed. Louis didn't argue with me about going back and forth to the doctors in Gary.

Louis was a carpenter and hadn't had any jobs in a long time. One day he was really depressed about this and he was feeling down on himself. He grabbed his rifle and told me that he was going out to the woods and that he was going to kill himself. Aunt Lillian and her husband owned the land that the cottage was on and their house was nearby. I ran to their house to tell someone. His uncle was home and he went out to the woods to look for Louis. He found him and talked to him. He convinced him not to hurt himself. I was aware of all that he was putting me through, but I didn't want him to die. I still loved him.

Louis eventually found work, but it wasn't steady. He was doing odd jobs here and there. It was difficult to pay our bills, so I decided that I would look for work. Lillian said that she would babysit Terri if I found a job. I got a job as a machine operator on an assembly line. I still wasn't driving, so one of my co-workers would pick me up and take me to work.

When I was further along in my pregnancy, I had to go on maternity leave. I wanted our own home. I thought that if we had a place that we could call our own, a place that would keep us busy, maybe things would get better.

Chapter 4

The president of the company that I was working for loaned me the money to purchase a house in Covert, Michigan, which is 12 miles east of Bangor. Pete Watson, the man selling it, was from Chicago. He had purchased this section of land from the Wilsons, who owned 90 acres of land. We bought the 1-acre property from Pete for $6,000.

It was a white 1-story house with 2 bedrooms and it was fully furnished. Pete said that he no longer needed the things inside. He had purchased the home for him and his wife to be used as a vacation home. His wife had passed away and he decided that he no longer needed a vacation home.

Louis seemed to be happy about our new home and I felt that things were getting better. He had a genuine interest in cultivating the land and making it fertile. Louis gathered some soil and went to an agricultural specialist to have it analyzed. They informed him what to add to it to make it fertile, so we added lime to the soil and got to work.

Louis rented a tractor to plow the land and then he rented a hand cultivator. He plowed a garden area in the back yard and on the side of the house. We planted a vegetable garden in both locations. In the gardens we grew corn, beans, greens, eggplants, cucumbers, squash, cauliflower, onions, and potatoes. We also put some blueberry bushes, dwarf apple, and pear trees around the house.

Louis built a small green house attached to the house and that's where we would start our tomato and onion plants. Once they were big enough, we'd transfer them to the garden outside. This brought back some memories of my childhood. My mother would give me and my oldest brother a spot in her garden. We'd be responsible for planting and growing things in that area.

Gardening was always relaxing to me. I worked in the garden during the day pulling weeds and thinning out some areas. Some of the vegetables would grow too close together, so I had to thin them out by removing anything that would be in the way. We always had a good turnout. Sometimes the greens would grow really fast and had to be picked early.

When the vegetables were ready to be picked, I'd store a lot of them, and then give the rest away. I'd give some away to the church members and to the neighbors. Louis would give some away to his friends too.

In addition to growing vegetables, we raised pigs and rabbits. Louis built a pig pen and bought some pigs. We fed them until they got big enough, then Louis would take them to the packing house. He would come back with lots of food to put in the freezer. He decided to give a whole pig to his sister's new boyfriend, who was married. I always wondered why he did that.

There was a small barn that was on the property when we bought it. He used the barn to breed rabbits. Terri became really attached to them. One day Terri picked a rabbit up and shortly after it died. We didn't know that if humans touched rabbits when they are young, that they wouldn't survive.

On Sundays, Terri and I would go to church with the neighbors. Louis never went. I don't think he believed in the ministers by the way he would talk negative about them. Most of the ladies that I'd go to church with were much older than me. This was my time of comfort. I felt safe at church.

I met neighbors that were close to my age and we became friends. They'd give me rides to the grocery store. Louis couldn't stand for me to be with them. They would ask me to ride with them about 20 miles away to Benton Harbor, Michigan to visit their relatives. Louis didn't like that because they were my age and he wanted to choose my friends. He just wanted me to be friends with his friend's wives. We argued about this. I felt that I should have the friends that I wanted.

I cherished my time with Terri. We would play games and I'd read to her. We'd color and write. Terri was very smart and when she was 3 years old the school tested her and said that she was ready for 1st grade. The school explained that even though she was academically ready for 1st, that they didn't recommend putting her there being that young. We decided to start her in kindergarten instead. We started attending the school board meetings and Louis would speak out about his thoughts on how to improve the school system. Everyone would hang on his every word. They would comment on how good of a speaker he was. They saw the Louis that I fell in love with and as long as he was working he was ok because he was busy and not at home that much.

Mrs. Wilson introduced me to one of the other neighbors. She was a teacher's aide where Terri went to school. She owned a farm with a plum orchard on it and she said that I could have all the plums I wanted. That was, if I would teach her how to make plum preserves and jelly. People in town loved my blueberry preserves and jelly that I would make using the blueberries from the bushes at my house.

She came to my home and picked me up and I showed her the sure gel recipe that I often used and we canned. I only showed her once, but I was able to get plums from her whenever I wanted. Covert was a small farming community. Most of the farmers were Black and many of them had blueberry farms. I enjoyed canning as much as I enjoyed gardening, so I was delighted to add plum preserves to my pantry. I would also go to the strawberry farms and pick strawberries to can.

I was fed up with being chauffeured around and relying on others to take me places. I finally decided to get my driver's license, so I started taking driving lessons. My driving teacher would come to the house and pick me up for my lessons. When it was time to take the road test he came and got me. Luckily, I was able to use one of the vehicles that we would practice in. I passed and got my license, but Louis didn't want me to drive, so I still had to count on him and my neighbors to take me places.

Louis and I were sitting around talking about our families one day, when he started talking garbage about mine. He said that my sisters and brothers wouldn't amount to anything. He continued trash talking by saying that the reason my parents don't have anything is because they spend all their money buying things for kids. He was being really mean and ugly, so I said some bad things about his family too. I stated the facts that his sister was a prostitute and his brother was a drug dealer. he lost it. He got so mad that he jumped on me and I had to fight him off. He went to get the gun and he waved it in my face and put it in my mouth. He broke my glasses and I got away. I went to the phone and called the police. When the police arrived, they took his gun and left with it. I was glad that the gun was gone, but I was still felt threatened. Louis went to the station the next day and they gave him the gun back. His gun was registered so I guess they felt he should have it back. I did not feel at ease.

A couple weeks went by and we argued. He jumped on me and went and got the gun. I got loose and ran to get the phone to call the police and that's when he snatched the cord out the wall. All hope was lost. He got even more upset and put the gun in my mouth and from that day on I barely slept. Every night I would cry and pray that something would change. I tried to go home, but he came and got me. I tried to go to other relatives, but he came and got me. I tried the hospital, but he came and got me. I even tried the police, but they gave him his gun back. I began to feel like this was just something I had to accept and deal with.

Every time I thought things would get better, something happened to trigger his violence. He would tell me that no other man would ever want me. He drilled this into my head and I believed it. He threatened to take Terri and my unborn child away from me if I left him. I felt like my situation was past hope.

His sister and her kids had come to visit Lillian, so we took Terri over there to play with them. Someone threw a rock and smashed a car window. There were 3 older kids there and 4-year-old Terri. They accused Terri of throwing the rock and we had to pay for it. Louis was not happy about this at all. I attempted to reason with him. I tried to get him to understand that Terri was too little to throw a rock with that force. I pleaded with him to not whip her - that she was only 4 but her cousins were 8, 9, and 11. He didn't listen. He waited until she was taking a shower and he snatched her out of the shower and whipped her. This made me furious, so we started arguing, yelling, and then it got physical again. He went and got the gun and threatened me and held me while he put the gun in my mouth. I felt as though I didn't have a choice but to back down again. He took me to the hospital and told them I was mentally ill. I knew something was different about me. I was depressed and I had all kinds of emotions fighting in my head, but I was convinced that he was the one that was mentally ill.

Chapter 5

It was time to deliver my baby. Louis acted like he was happy when Carla was born and things appeared to be getting better. I was wrong. Carla had not turned one yet and she started to cry for some reason. Louis got real upset. He went and got her out of her crib, he took off his belt and whipped her and just like the times he would do this to Terri we ended up fighting. I had fears that the abuse would start again. I hit him with a lamp and he went and grabbed the gun and put it in my mouth and when he let go of me I ran and called the police. I was able to dial before he could yank the cord from the wall. He told me that if I said anything to the police when they got there, that he'd take the children and I'd never see them again.

When the police arrived, he told them that everything was okay. That evening he admitted me into the hospital again, saying that I was mentally deranged. I stayed for a few days. Wherever I went and tried to get away he came after me threatening me. There was no way out alive. I thought that because I had children that I would stay and deal with whatever the situation was. He made me believe that no one would ever want me because I had kids.

A couple of days after I got back from the hospital he came home and was upset about something that had happened at work. Without saying anything he grabbed his rifle and went outside. I heard several shots. I was scared for him, because I thought that he had shot himself. I rushed outside to the gruesome scene. I couldn't believe any of it. He had shot the rabbits, our beagle, our short haired pointer and our yard dog. My heart sank. Terri came out and saw the rabbits. She was horrified and cried uncontrollably as she ran back in the house. Louis and I argued as I attempted to make sense of what had just happened, but he just left and went to a bar.

We didn't talk when he got back late that night. I stayed awake until morning. I would've never thought that he would do what he did. He was unpredictable and I didn't know what else he was going to do. I couldn't get the images of the dead animals out of my head. The next morning, he got up and went to work like nothing happened.

When he comes back from work, he's outside looking at our dead rabbits and dogs pacing back and forth. I'm walking out of the house to where he is to ask him why. Why? I keep asking why he did what he did. Why? He's not giving me a reason, but he's getting upset. I want to understand why he killed them. How do I explain this to our kids? They will not understand. I do not understand. We're arguing, we're both screaming and yelling. I still don't know why. I see him look at the door to the house and then back at the dead animals and then to me with an evil look on his face. Oh no! What is he going to do next? Is he going to do what he did to the animals to me and the children? I know I made the covenant until death do us part, but I didn't want that death to be mine or my girls. Things were happening so quickly. I think he's going to get the gun. I dart inside the house and I grab the gun then hurry back outside. We're still yelling at each other. I have the gun; the tables have turned. He can't go get it and threaten me and put it in my mouth. I take the 38 automatic and I raise it in the air. I want to shoot in the air to scare him. Maybe he'll back down.

He's coming at me and he's trying to get the gun. My heart is pounding and I'm panicking. The fear that I'm feeling is far worse than any other time. He's grabbing my hand. We're struggling! The gun goes off. It shoots him in the hand. He's running and the gun is still firing. I blackout.

Chapter 6

I saw him lying on the ground. I ran inside the house and called the police. I told them that Louis was shot. I added that Terri and Carla were in the house. The police arrived and I was in shock. I couldn't remember what had just happened. I was mentally drained and wasn't able to express any emotions. The police asked me to call someone to come and get my girls. I called a neighbor and she kept them until my brothers could get them and take them to my mother's house. The police took me to jail.

One of my brothers bailed me out the next day and got me a lawyer. While out on bail I went back to my house to await trial. I couldn't believe what had happened there. I felt dejected. I missed my children and I was feeling alone.

There was a funeral for Louis and two of my neighbors went. They didn't like Louis, but they went anyway. They said that there weren't many people there. I wondered, how did this ever happen?

I didn't think that my girls knew what was going on, but after my mother told me that something wasn't right with Carla, I realized that maybe they did sense that something terrible had happened. I prayed that this would not ruin their lives. My mother took Carla to the doctor and he said that everything was ok, but that she seemed anxious. I felt pretty lonesome and I didn't want it to be a burden for my mother to keep the children. My aunt Evelyn convinced me that it would be good for my mother. I felt remorseful about everything that had happened. I was 29 and I didn't feel that I would have much of a future. I was thankful for my aunts because they were very encouraging to me. Aunt Evelyn assured me that I would have a future.

While awaiting trial, I got a job working with the youth in a summer camp and I helped my neighbors with their farms. After a couple of weeks my lawyer suggested that I go get a psychiatric evaluation because I was still showing signs of depression.

I went and stayed in a group home where people were being analyzed by a psychiatrist. I was feeling very lonely until I met a few people that were in similar situations. I met a lady who was more lonesome than I was. She would often ask me if I would play games with her or watch TV with her. We'd have group meetings at the home and I can remember that everyone there was always nice to me. I remember telling the psychiatrist during one of our individual sessions that I still had love for my husband. He said, "How could you still have love for someone who was so mean and cruel to you?" I couldn't answer that question then.

The evaluation took about a month and then the psychiatrist told the judge that I was ready for trial. I was in the courtroom with my lawyer, my parents, and one of my brothers. Louis' sister and his father were there too. My lawyer had asked aunt Lillian to tell the judge about the day that she saved Louis from killing me. She said the she wouldn't do that. The police officers that took the gun from Louis recounted that day to the judge.

The judge said that I seemed like a nice person but that I should not have had a gun. He sentenced me to 3-15 years for involuntary manslaughter. Louis' father said to me "just remember I'm still your dad". His sister didn't say a word. They knew that the children would be staying with my mother and they said that they would keep up with them. They never did. Nobody, me, my mother, or the girls ever heard anything from them since that day.

I was sad to leave my children behind, but I was thankful that the judge didn't give me more time. They sent me to the old prison in Detroit, Michigan for a little while. The state was building a new prison near Ann Arbor, about an hour west of Detroit. After about a month in Detroit I was transferred to the new facility. At both prisons I was in minimum security, so we were allowed to leave for approved reasons. I worked in the clinic and as a police aid while at the prison. In the mornings, I'd leave to go to school half of the day and the other half I worked in a mentally handicap school, both in were in Plymouth, Michigan. The prison had a bus that would take us to Plymouth and bring us back. My grades were so good in school that the teachers said I could go to college if I wanted to. I didn't believe that. I didn't even think that I could find good employment with a record.

Every month my aunt would send me $15 and she'd write me. I'd write my mom, but she didn't like to write, so I didn't receive letters from her. I'd call my mom collect and check on the children. I was embarrassed and ashamed, so I didn't talk to the kids much. I didn't want them to know where I was, even though they came out a few times to see me. I took bible classes and went to church. It was my faith that helped me through it. It also helped that I was able to keep my mind occupied by staying busy; there were lots of activities offered.

I think a lot of the other inmates there were jealous because I was an aid to the police matron. The matron was real nice to me, she'd bring me food from home sometimes. One day an inmate tried to start an argument with me and then came at me. I had a pencil in my hand and I raised the pencil back to scare her hoping that she wouldn't try to jump on me. It worked and I was relieved that she left me alone.

I was released after 18 months. During probation, I had to stay in the state of Michigan, so I went to Lansing, MI and worked as a maid in a hotel while staying at the YMCA. They let me transfer my probation to Milwaukee after about I year.

I was missing my girls. I talked to my lawyer and I asked him if I should get my children to move with me and he said "absolutely". One of my brothers brought my kids to Milwaukee. I was so happy to have them back. My mother suggested that I ask my aunt Gwen if we could stay with her and thankfully she said yes. My girls and I stayed with her for 3 weeks and I worked in a hotel as a maid. During that time, I had put in applications almost everywhere to find a better paying job. I finally got a call from Allen Bradley, an electric company, and went to work there. We moved out of my aunt's place into an apartment. I started saving and after 3 months I was able to buy my own house. Soon after that I paid my brother and my lawyer back. I was feeling really hopeful about the future.

Epilogue

I'm thankful that God saved me and preserved my life in order for me to take care of my children. I was able to put my girls in private school. They both graduated early from high school. They graduated from college and have had successful careers. But what gives me the most joy are my beautiful grandchildren that they've blessed me with.

I feel that God has forgiven me, and I have forgiven him [Louis]. That is how I can still love him.

If you are going through a similar situation I would suggest that you leave and not go back. If you're afraid, like in my case, go to a shelter where you can have protection.

The National Domestic Violence Hotline
1-800-799-SAFE (7233)

TURNED TABLES: MEMOIRS OF A SURVIVOR

Made in the USA
Coppell, TX
28 March 2022